FRANCIS FRITH'S
TOWN & CITY
MEMORIES

HARLOW

CLARE BASTER was born in London and first got to know Harlow when she visited it with a cycling club. She was a primary school teacher in Harlow for fifteen years and got to know the town very well. Clare now lives in Epping and is helping to collect historical material for The Epping Map Project.

Harlow, River Stort c1955 H22012

FRANCIS FRITH'S
TOWN & CITY
MEMORIES

HARLOW

CLARE BASTER

The author and publisher gratefully acknowledge
the assistance of Mr David Devine and staff at
The Museum of Harlow in the production of this book

FRANCIS FRITH'S
TOWN & CITY
MEMORIES

First published as Harlow, A Photographic History of your Town
in 2002 by Black Horse Books, an imprint of The Francis Frith Collection
Revised edition published in the United Kingdom in 2006 by
The Francis Frith Collection as Harlow, Town and City Memories
Limited Hardback Edition ISBN 1-84589-117-1
Paperback Edition ISBN 1-84589-116-3

Text and Design copyright © The Francis Frith Collection®
Photographs copyright © The Francis Frith Collection®
except where indicated

The Frith® photographs and the Frith® logo are reproduced under licence from
Heritage Photographic Resources Ltd, the owners of the Frith® archive and trademarks.
'The Francis Frith Collection', 'Francis Frith' and 'Frith' are registered trademarks of Heritage
Photographic Resources Ltd.

All rights reserved. No photograph in this publication may be sold to a third party other
than in the original form of this publication, or framed for sale to a third party.
No parts of this publication may be reproduced, stored in a retrieval system, or transmitted,
in any form, or by any means, electronic, mechanical, photocopying, recording or otherwise,
without the prior permission of the publishers and copyright holder

British Library Cataloguing in Publication Data

Harlow
Town and City Memories
Clare Baster

The Francis Frith Collection®
Frith's Barn, Teffont,
Salisbury, Wiltshire SP3 5QP
Tel: +44 (0) 1722 716 376
Email: info@francisfrith.co.uk
www.francisfrith.co.uk

Aerial photographs reproduced under licence from Simmons Aerofilms Limited
Historical Ordnance Survey maps reproduced under licence from Homecheck.co.uk

Printed and bound in England

Front Cover: **HARLOW, THE FORD 1903** 51093t
The colour-tinting in this image is for illustrative purposes only,
and is not intended to be historically accurate

Every attempt has been made to contact copyright holders of illustrative material.
We will be happy to give full acknowledgement in future editions for any items not credited.
Any information should be directed to The Francis Frith Collection.

AS WITH ANY HISTORICAL DATABASE, THE FRANCIS FRITH ARCHIVE IS CONSTANTLY BEING
CORRECTED AND IMPROVED, AND THE PUBLISHERS WOULD WELCOME INFORMATION ON
OMISSIONS OR INACCURACIES

FRANCIS FRITH'S
Town & City
MEMORIES

Contents

The Making of an Archive	6
Harlow From the Air	8
Harlow Old Town, New Town	10
The River Stort and Harlow Mill	14
Old Harlow - The High Street	16
Old Harlow - The George and Harlow College	20
Mulberry Green	24
The Ford at Harlow	26
Old Harlow - New Settlers	28
Ordnance Survey Map	36
Potter Street	38
Essex County Map	46
The New Town	48
The Stow	50
Treasures of the Past	52
The Neighbourhood Clusters	56
The Town Centre	60
The Market Square	66
The Railway - Harlow Station	71
The Civic Centre	74
New Churches and Public Buildings	78
Names of Subscribers	86
Index	87

VOUCHER FOR FREE MOUNTED PRINT   89

The Making of an Archive

Francis Frith, Victorian founder of the world-famous photographic archive, was a devout Quaker and a highly successful Victorian businessman. By 1860 he was already a multi-millionaire, having established and sold a wholesale grocery business in Liverpool. He had also made a series of pioneering photographic journeys to the Nile region. The images he returned with were the talk of London. An eminent modern historian has likened their impact on the population of the time to that on our own generation of the first photographs taken on the surface of the moon.

Frith had a passion for landscape, and was as equally inspired by the countryside of Britain as he was by the desert regions of the Nile. He resolved to set out on a new career and to use his skills with a camera. He established a business in Reigate as a specialist publisher of topographical photographs.

Frith lived in an era of immense and sometimes violent change. For the poor in the early part of Victoria's reign work was a drudge and the hours long, and ordinary people had precious little free time. Most had not travelled far beyond the boundaries of their own town or village. Mass tourism was in its infancy during the 1860s, but during the next decade the railway network and the establishment of Bank Holidays and half-Saturdays gradually made it possible for the working man and his family to enjoy holidays and to see a little more of the world. With characteristic business acumen, Francis Frith foresaw that these new tourists would enjoy having souvenirs to commemorate their days out. He began selling photo-souvenirs of seaside resorts and beauty spots, which the Victorian public pasted into treasured family albums.

Frith's aim was to photograph every town and village in Britain. For the next thirty years he travelled the country by train and by pony and trap, producing fine photographs of seaside resorts and beauty spots that were keenly bought by millions of Victorians.

The Rise of Frith & Co

Each photograph was taken with tourism in mind, the small team of Frith photographers concentrating on busy shopping streets, beaches, seafronts, picturesque lanes and villages. They also photographed buildings: the Victorian and Edwardian eras were times of huge building activity, and town halls, libraries, post offices, schools and technical colleges were springing up all over the country. They were invariably celebrated by a proud Victorian public, and photo souvenirs – visual records – published by F Frith & Co were sold in their hundreds of thousands. In addition, many new commercial buildings such as hotels, inns and pubs were photographed, often because their owners specifically commissioned Frith postcards or prints of them for re-sale or for publicity purposes.

In order to gain some understanding of the scale of Frith's business one only has to look at the catalogue issued by Frith & Co in 1886: it runs to some 670 pages. By 1890 Frith had created the greatest specialist photographic publishing company in the world, with over 2,000 stockists! The picture on the right shows the Frith & Co display board on the wall of the stockist at Ingleton in the Yorkshire Dales (left of window). Beautifully constructed with a mahogany frame and gilt inserts, it displayed a dozen scenes.

FRANCIS FRITH: THE MAKING OF AN ARCHIVE

Postcard Bonanza

The ever-popular holiday postcard we know today took many years to appear, and F Frith & Co was in the vanguard of its development. Postcards became a hugely popular means of communication and sold in their millions. Frith's company took full advantage of this boom and soon became the major publisher of photographic view postcards.

Francis Frith died in 1898 at his villa in Cannes, his great project still growing. His sons Eustace and Cyril continued their father's monumental task, expanding the number of views offered to the public and recording more and more places in Britain, as the coasts and countryside were opened up to mass travel. The archive Frith created continued in business for another seventy years. By 1970 it contained over a third of a million pictures of 7,000 cities, towns and villages. The massive photographic record Frith has left to us stands as a living monument to a special and very remarkable man.

This book shows Harlow as it was photographed by this world-famous archive at various periods in its development over the past 150 years. Every photograph was taken for a specific commercial purpose, which explains why the selection may not show every aspect of the town landscape. However, the photographs, compiled from one of the world's most celebrated archives, provide an important and absorbing record of your town.

HARLOW FROM THE AIR

HARLOW FROM THE AIR

Harlow from the Air AFA75174

HARLOW OLD TOWN, NEW TOWN

THE little village of Harlow has evidence of Bronze Age, Iron Age, Roman and Saxon occupation. The location, by the river amid good farming land, made it a good place for settlements. Tools and burials from the Bronze Age have been found in the area known now as Temple Hill on the banks of the River Stort.

Another important site is at Gilden Way, where evidence suggests a fairly large settlement. Thurstan, a Saxon thane, said on his deathbed: 'I give the land at Harlow to St Edmunds, except the half-hide which Alfwine had at Gildenbridge'. Gildenbridge is now Ealing Bridge, while Gilden has been used to name the new road that leads to it. The temple site on Stanegrove Hill was also used in Iron Age times. Coins, tools, weapons, bones and pottery were found there when Harlow Mill Station was being built. The Romans found Old Harlow very important militarily, as it overlooked the River Stort and the Roman river crossing of the road between Bishop's Stortford and Chigwell. They developed the Temple Hill site, building their own temple. Excavations have found ornaments, coins, shoes, glass, pottery, and stone heads of Minerva and Bacchus. Some coffins were found when Harlow Station was built in 1841, which have been reburied.

It is now known that the origin of the name 'Harlow' was 'Hill of the Temple', and a Saxon tumulus in Harlow called Mudborrow, from the Saxon words 'mot beorgh' meaning 'meeting place', is now known as Mulberry Green. The Norman Conquest brought many changes, and the careful listing in the Domesday book of every person (268 of them), animal and piece of land in the parish. Each parish had its owners, but most unusually one was held by a Aelfeva, a free woman.

Harlowbury Norman chapel, a Grade I listed building situated in Old Road, appears to be Norman, but in fact there is evidence of a much earlier building. From the position of the post-holes it is known that the timber building was inside the rubble structure, and the later had three crown-post trusses. It was part of the Abbey lands from between 1044-1539. The chapel was used as a grain store until recently, and there are plans to use the chapel for educational and community use. The private residence behind is even more interesting: the 19th-century brick exterior encloses a 13th-century timber-framed abbot's palace. There were many manorial rights held by the abbots, including the mill. In the 13th century, they claimed a toll of one penny from carts crossing the bridge.

The abbots at Harlowbury were responsible for appointing a vicar for the parish, which carried an endowment. The parish church was St Mary's in Churchgate Street. The vicarage that is used now was the old Rectory House until 1398. The Norman church of St Mary was largely rebuilt at this time, and added St Hugh to its name (51094, pages 12-13).

Harlow, Latton, Netteswell, Great Parndon and Little Parndon were five adjacent parishes stretching southwards up a slope from the River Stort in the north. Harlow was the most developed of the villages with shops and businesses, while the others were mainly agricultural. There have been many changes to these areas, but the mills and mill pools have not been disturbed. The roads, tracks and paths were similar to those used in the New Town. The turnpike road from Epping to Stortford, completed between 1828 and 1841, followed the line of old roads as far as the George at Old Harlow. An

HARLOW OLD TOWN, NEW TOWN

OLD HARLOW, CHURCHGATE STREET 1903 51086

Churchgate Street lay on the main route from London to Newmarket, Cambridge, Norwich and the North. Until early in the 19th century, travellers in horse-drawn carriages from London would see the welcome sight of the Queen's Head and the spire of the church of St Mary and St Hugh in the background as they rounded the bend in the road. Stafford Almshouse, now privately owned, was originally the home of a priest until 1548, when it became an almshouse for 'two poor widows to be given 20s for wood and 20s for clothing every year'. Anyone standing on this same spot now would find that Churchgate Street looks almost the same now as in the photograph.

extension of this road, from the George through a fairground and across a large demesne of ploughed land called Millfield and then down to the mill, was added later. The River Stort was canalised in 1769, and this brought trade and work to Harlow. Then in 1841 the Northern and Eastern Railway was extended. A station, now known as Harlow Mill, was built, and this ruined the river trade.

When Sir Frederick Gibberd was appointed in 1946 to design Harlow New Town, he decided to rename Harlow village Old Harlow, and to keep it almost as it was. The new town would be built on the other four villages to the west of Old Harlow, preserving names, lanes, churches, mills, pubs and other 'treasures of the past'. The New Town was to have a beautiful townscape, with wide tree-lined roads, dense planting of trees and shrubs, and deliberate use of

HARLOW OLD TOWN, NEW TOWN

the existing landscape to be left in wedges, or linear parks, to separate the new neighbourhood clusters. Uninteresting areas would be used as playing fields and open spaces. The industrial units which were planned to make Harlow self-sufficient were to be on the outskirts of the town set in landscaped areas, within easy reach of the houses.

Harlow New Town, part of a long-term plan to build eight new towns round London, was planned to ease the housing crisis after the Second World War. Many people from the East End of London had lost their homes in the blitz, and moving to Harlow New Town was a good way to make a new start. The town was to house a well-paid industrial population, to have a balanced age structure, and to be self-contained. Only those who worked in Harlow could be rehoused there.

THE CHURCH OF ST MARY AND ST HUGH, CHURCHGATE STREET 1903 51094

The church of St Mary and St Hugh was badly damaged by fire in 1708, which burnt down the spire and melted the bells. When the church was rebuilt a dome was constructed over the crossing and a new bell tower at the west end. While the work was going on, a small iron chest was unearthed, inscribed in Latin 'St Catherine's blood'. A 13th-century stained glass window depicting the Virgin and Child was saved, and has remained intact through many alterations. The church has the largest collection of brasses in any Essex church.

HARLOW OLD TOWN, NEW TOWN

THE RIVER STORT AND HARLOW MILL

THE RIVER STORT AND HARLOW MILL

THE MILL 1903 51092

The 17th-century mill at Harlow was part of the manor of Harlowbury. It was the main source of power to grind corn and other purposes for the parish at that time. There was a supply of fresh water that was pumped from wells nearby.

DURING the Saxon period, water mills were shared by everyone in the village. There were several mills on the Stort: Harlow (51092, opposite) was built before the 12th century; Parndon Mill's original date is not known, but it was rebuilt further downstream in the 13th century following difficulties caused by Netteswell Mill, built in 1190. Latton Mill ceased working in 1926, while Parndon Mill was the last operating mill in Harlow and finally ceased working in the late 1950s. In the reign of Henry II windmills began to be built, but they were less powerful than the watermills. The monks at Harlow took over one of the windmills - its profit was 20s compared with that of the watermill, which was 100s.

The Stort Navigation Company canalised the river between 1766 and 1769, and soon huge horse-drawn barges were taking goods to London. The barges were preferred to coaches for carrying goods, as the roads were so bad. Trade was good both ways. The main cargo from Harlow was malt and barley for London's beer - the local malting and brewing industry was an important source of work and income for Harlow. Coal and a variety of goods from London were unloaded at Harlow Mill (51092, opposite) and taken by horse and cart up through Mulberry Green for delivery to shops and businesses by a local man known as 'Barge Billy'.

In 1836 The Northern and Eastern Company began building a railway, which reached Harlow by 1841. The company intended the railway to take away the freight traffic from the canal, and this was exactly what happened. The Reverend Joseph Arkwright was a major landowner. He did much to improve the life of his parishioners who depended to a large extent on trade and work related to the canal. He did not think the railway would be a good thing - he even tried to petition

THE RIVER STORT AND HARLOW MILL

Parliament to stop the Bill going through. However he was unsuccessful, and finally accepted £7,800 for the land. The canal and locks deteriorated until 1924, when they were repaired, and the waterways were reopened for river traffic and pleasure boating. Harlow Mill is now a country pub pleasantly situated beside a meandering river by the bridge that crosses from Essex into Hertfordshire.

There is a footpath by the hotel which leads to the site of the Roman temple in an industrial area called Templefields.

OLD HARLOW - THE HIGH STREET

OLD HARLOW COTTAGES c1955 H22015

Seventy-nine Old Harlow residents were very resistant to selling their property to the corporation. However, finally everyone was persuaded, and the work went ahead.

THE HIGH STREET (51087, pages 18-19) was once known as 'the way to the church'. It backed onto a rough grassy area called Mark Hall Moors, which is nowadays included in Mark Hall Park. In medieval times the village was an important coaching station, with a junction to Newmarket in the north and Sheering in the east.

After the development of the New Town, the increased traffic in the High Street became intolerable. It was later

OLD HARLOW - THE HIGH STREET

and Market Street, most of the houses in the High Street were occupied by smallholders who rented strips of land in an area called chipping field (market field) nearby. These men were known as mil men or mol men, as they paid rent for their smallholdings, unlike the villeins who paid in labour or goods. Later, shops were opened with people living above them. There is a nine-bay Georgian house in the High Street which was later used as a bank, and several other later Georgian buildings. Old Harlow had a telephone exchange in 1910, first of all in Read's shop, and later at Mr Beard's house in New Road. The automatic exchange did not open until 1965.

When the Development Corporation looked at the area, they found an attractive village that was in serious decline. It had once been self-sufficient, but now shoppers were going farther afield. In 1957 a plan was approved for the redevelopment of the old town which included pedestrianisation of short lengths of the High Street. The architect of the scheme was Frederick Gibberd, who was awarded a Civic Trust award for the scheme. Properties were bought by the corporation, and leased back to traders. Old buildings were carefully reconstructed (H22015, left), new ones were carefully inserted, and finally the whole area was pedestrianised. The project gained three prestigious awards.

relieved by two new roads, the A414 from London to East Anglia, and the B183 from Harlow to Hatfield.

The High Street was originally in an area called Market Plain. Unlike the other streets, Fore Street

OLD HARLOW - THE HIGH STREET

OLD HARLOW - THE HIGH STREET

Old Harlow, High Street 1903 51087

The road to Harlow was a turnpike costing 1s for a coach and horses, and 1d for a horse. The eight daily coaches would have passed the Bull and Horseshoes near Potter Street, the Queen's Head at Churchgate Street, the Green Man near Mulberry Green and the George at the end of the High Street. The road then led down to Harlow Mill on the Stort and the bridge into Hertfordshire.

OLD HARLOW - THE GEORGE AND HARLOW COLLEGE

A MEDIEVAL MAP shows six streets in Old Harlow: Hoo Street (now known as Old Road), Moteburgh Street, Yeldenbregge, Churchgate Street, Foster Street, and Potter Street. All of these names are still in use in some form or other.

Travellers to London, having crossed the bridge by the Mill, would go up Old Road, past Harlowbury Chapel, through Mulberry Green on into Churchgate Street, and then across country to Mill Street and Hastingwood, or across Harlow Common at Potter Street to join the present London Road, where they might stop at the Bull and Horseshoes (now a McDonalds). The road to the Bull and Horseshoes was so steep that in 1828 the crown of the road was lowered nine feet. Later a turnpike road was constructed to bypass Churchgate Street and Mulberry Green and go straight through Old Harlow to Potter Street. A final stretch from the George to the mill was later added on, cutting through a medieval fair ground (land later occupied by Barclays Bank) and Mill Field.

The George was the scene of many public events. Fairs and shows took place there, and in 1905 everyone turned out to see King Edward VII go through the mud of

OLD HARLOW, THE GEORGE 1903 51089

The George, built in 1598, was situated at the junction between the High Street, Market Street, and Fore Street, and was the main focal point of the village.

OLD HARLOW - THE GEORGE AND HARLOW COLLEGE

Station Road on his way to the Newmarket races. Over the years peopled gathered there to hear the result of General Elections, especially the one when Winston Churchill was returned as their member - he remained so until 1945. It was the responsibility of each parish to provide a lock-up with stocks and a whipping post, and Harlow's Old Cage (a village lock-up) and the stocks were in the lower yard at the George. The victim sat on a three-legged stool and became 'the laughing stock'.

Opposite the George is a 15th-century house with a pretty Georgian doorway; its timbers are exposed today, and it is currently a restaurant. The George traded as a pub until 1948, then various businesses took it over, including a dress shop and a haberdashery store. To the right of the George and a little way down the road is a single-gabled house where Mr Samuel Deards and his family lived (51089, page 20). The house was called The Welcome, and on New Year's Eve 1877 it was the scene of a wonderful party, called Ye Olde Couples Treat – given for many years by the Deards until 1888, after which it was held annually at Victoria Hall, St John's Road, Old Harlow. Sam Deards was the son of a local plumber and glazier. While working for his father, he invented a dry glaze method of using glass which was used in Liverpool Street Station and the Crystal Palace. He also played cricket at Mulberry Green; becoming irritated by the method of scoring, he invented the type of scoreboard used everywhere today.

OLD HARLOW, THE COLLEGE 1903 51091

Harlow College was situated in the area now known as Jocelyns. It was originally called St Mary's, and was planned to be a boarding school for fifty middle-class boys. It was closed in 1964 and demolished in 1965.

OLD HARLOW - THE GEORGE AND HARLOW COLLEGE

Harlow College (51091, page 20, and 51090, right) was built in 1862 at a cost of £3,000, and was to provide an education based on the principles of the Church of England. St John's church was nearby and the pupils attended a service every day.

Originally known as St Mary's, the school was later called Harlow College, and accepted boys awarded scholarships by Essex County Council. In the 1950s, with one hundred and fifty boys attending, the school was closed. Later, Harlow College was demolished, and the site was subsequently sold to Harlow Development Corporation.

St John's church was built in 1839 in the Gothic revival style. It was declared redundant in 1979, and is now an arts centre. There is a link with St John's teacher training college, Newfoundland: the students come over for periods of three to six months, staying at The Maltings. They are then allocated a school, where they work alongside the teacher and study their teaching methods.

OLD HARLOW, THE COLLEGE 1903 51090

The college was in a lovely setting, and was within walking distance of the river, where the boys were taken for swimming lessons. This view now would include houses on the field and the school area. St John's church is in the background.

OLD HARLOW - THE GEORGE AND HARLOW COLLEGE

MULBERRY GREEN

OLD HARLOW, MULBERRY GREEN c1920 H22014

The 15th-century Green Man is possibly Old Harlow's oldest pub. With the forge next door (left), it was an important staging post for coaches travelling from London to East Anglia or the North. Many coach routes started and finished here. The new turnpike road that was built bypassing Mulberry Green destroyed the trade catering for the coach passengers. The forge was very important during the coaching era, and was still working in the 1920s, but it is no longer operating, and is now a private house.

MULBERRY GREEN

MULBERRY GREEN

ALTHOUGH the passing trade brought by the stagecoaches declined, Mulberry Green remained a busy gathering place, with fairs, carnivals and the local hunt. A mulberry tree was planted in 1901 to mark the coronation of Edward VII, and another one was planted for our present Queen in 1952. Samuel Young and Sons was the largest shop in Old Harlow, selling and delivering high quality food and supplies.

In 1877 a fire engine was bought by public subscription for £278, and a volunteer fire brigade was formed. Sam Deards, a local businessman, was the captain of the brigade, and kept the fire engine near to his home, The Welcome, opposite The George (51089, pages 20). This was against the wishes of the chairman of the Parish Council, William Coleman, who wanted it kept in the fire engine house, which had been built in Mulberry Green. Deards' brigade went to fifty-four fires over the next thirty years at very little cost to Harlow, but the quarrel went on for years, and finally reached the national press. There was even a suggestion that Harlow's fires should be attended by Epping Fire Brigade.

The dispute ended in 1917 when the fire engine was required by the War Office to pump out the trenches in France. The engine house is still there, right next door to the ambulance station, which was built and maintained with money raised at a carnival held every August from 1929 to 1939. The carnival was probably held on Marigolds, the grassy area behind the Green Man; it was donated by Mr Geoffrey Hoare, and held in trust for the people of Harlow for ever.

THE FORD AT HARLOW

THE FORD AT HARLOW

THE FORD AT HARLOW

OLD HARLOW, THE FORD 1903 51093

HARLOW FORD could be found where the road crossed the Harlowbury Brook on the Sheering road from Harlow to Hatfield Heath. When the brook was in full spate, horses and carts would have had to go through water that reached the top of the horses' legs. In 1904, one year after the photograph was taken, Essex County Council improved the road as part of their road programme and built a bridge over the brook. This road has now been bypassed by Gilden Way as part of the new town plan.

The boys in 51093 (left) are all identically dressed, which suggests that they were attending one of the schools that had started in Harlow, such as Harlow College, Fawbert and Barnard, William Martin's school for poor children, a seminary for young men, and several church schools. In 1864 a curious little clock tower was built by Mr Arkwright. The building and its inscription, 'Work while it is day', can be seen from the main road (the A414) near Potter Street. The clock was intended to make sure his workers came on time, but Arkwright also set up a little school in the building opposite. The fees were 1d a week, although some children were allowed to bring an egg instead. The school lasted from 1848 to 1911.

The large building in the photograph on the left is the Police Station, built in 1852 by a local businessman, Mr Watlington. In 1852 he also built a reformatory for young men at Harlow Tye. It held twenty pupils and closed in 1879.

OLD HARLOW - NEW SETTLERS

OLD HARLOW - NEW SETTLERS

THE Development Corporation was anxious to make a start, and in 1949 the first houses in the New Town were built in Old Road, and these were soon followed by ninety-eight houses at Chippingfield (H22017, pages 34-35) and more at The Green (H22013, pages 30-31). The new settlers at that time were mainly construction workers, carpenters, plumbers and people with all the other skills involved in house and road building.

H22021 (pages 32-33) shows the Post Office in Station Road, roughly six years after the first developments in Old Harlow. The little country street used to be the main route to East Anglia, with the George (the tall building in the background) the centre of village life. The young woman waiting at the bus stop is probably from London, and has been rehoused in Old Harlow. There were plenty of shops in Old Harlow for her to go to, but she was probably suffering from loneliness and boredom, which was quite common among young New Town women at that time. It was possible to get buses to the town centre, and Harlow Mill Station was just a short walk away for a trip back home to London.

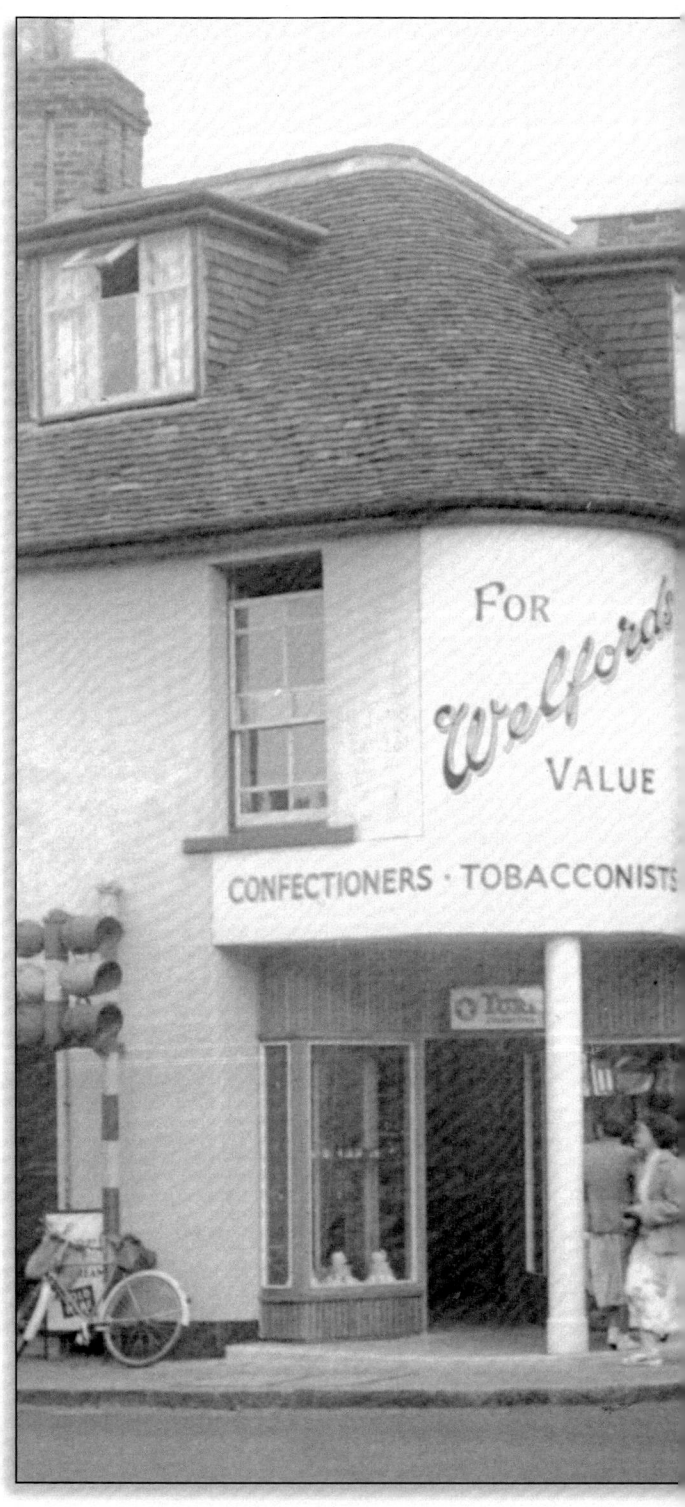

OLD HARLOW, WELFORDS CORNER C1955 H22026

Here we see a traditional corner shop and general grocery store.

OLD HARLOW - NEW SETTLERS

OLD HARLOW - NEW SETTLERS

OLD HARLOW - NEW SETTLERS

OLD HARLOW, THE GREEN C1955 H22013

The spacious open nature of this estate was typical of the style of all the new building. However, the lack of garages was later to cause problems.

OLD HARLOW - NEW SETTLERS

OLD HARLOW - NEW SETTLERS

Old Harlow, Post Office Corner c1955 H22021

OLD HARLOW - NEW SETTLERS

OLD HARLOW - NEW SETTLERS

OLD HARLOW, THE CHIPPINGFIELD HOUSING AREA c1955 H22017

The Chippingfield housing area was one of the first to be built by the Development Corporation. In the 13th century the site had been a market-field ('chipping field'), which was rented and worked by smallholders known as mol men from the rent they paid.

ORDNANCE SURVEY MAP

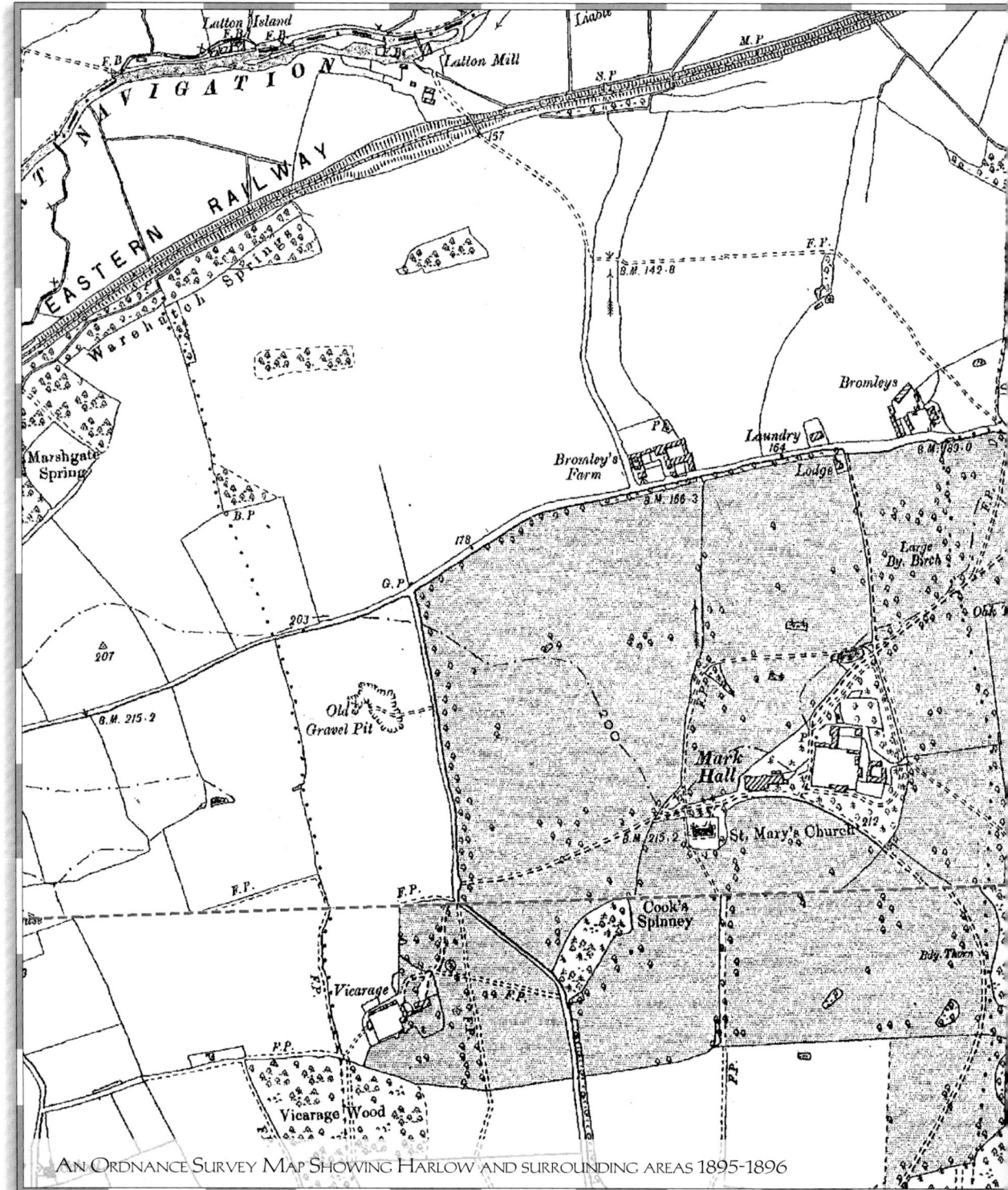

An Ordnance Survey Map showing Harlow and surrounding areas 1895-1896

HARLOW ORDNANCE SURVEY MAP

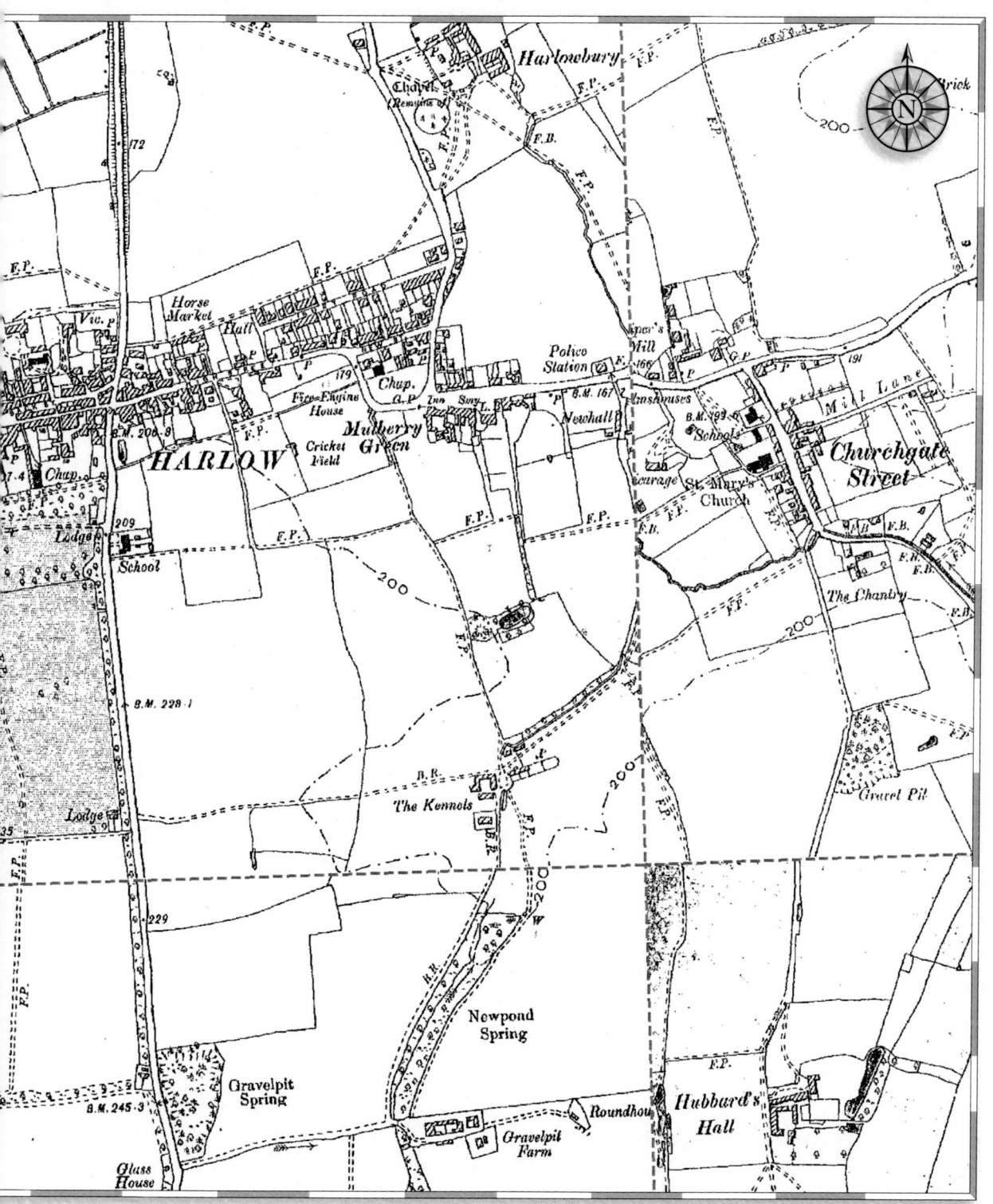

POTTER STREET

POTTER STREET

POTTER STREET (P147005, opposite) is principally known for pottery from the Tudor period. The clay was dug from Harlow Common, which caused a great deal of trouble if the holes were not filled in properly, or if the potter's kiln had become delapidated.

The Wright family were in business here for many generations, and later in the early 17th century the Prentice family (note Prentice Place, to the right in P147005) came to Potter Street and began operating two kilns. They were in business until the mid 18th century, when the pottery industry declined. The clay was made into a variety of household items, decorated products known as Metropolitan ware, and later tiles and bricks; it was mainly for local use, until the canal was opened for traffic and the roads improved in the 18th century - then the yellow and brown goods could be sold in London. The industry was completely finished by 1891, and Harlow Common is now a large green expanse for everyone's use.

POTTER STREET, PRENTICE PLACE C1955 P147005

This is the new parade of shops built by Harlow Development Corporation. Dorringtons (right) is a local baker with several shops in and around Harlow. Welfords, the general store of Old Harlow (H22026, page 25) has a corner site. The Red Lion next to Prentice Place (centre right) has 17th- and 18th-century features behind later additions. During the Second World War, the Red Lion was an ARP post. The empty roads were typical of the day - at this time, cars and garages had not yet become an important factor in the new estates. The King's Head was demolished two years after this photograph was taken.

HARLOW
POTTER STREET

HARLOW
POTTER STREET

The Sun and Whalebone was built in 1732, and rebuilt in 1935; its forecourt was decorated with monster whalebones. It was the headquarters of the Essex Hunt, and several horses belonging to London members were stabled there. One keen follower of the Essex Hunt was Anthony Trollope. There is a very good description of the Sun and Whalebone in his book 'Can You Forgive Her?'. The Gatekeeper, a Beefeater restaurant, opened in the 1990s on the site of the pub.

In Trollope's description of the area he refers to 'St Mary Magdalene's church in its lovely setting of trees and open grassland'. This was probably the very pretty church that was gradually rebuilt in its present form (P147009, right).

When bicycles and motorcycles began to be used for leisure, there were rallies at the Sun and Whalebone, and Potter Street became a favourite place for refreshment or an overnight stop. There was a receiving office in the village, and later a post office, which is now a private house. Dent's was a general store, and they were agents for Gilbeys' wines and spirits. The shop carried on trading in the 1950s when New Town development had already begun in the village.

The White Horse (P147001, pages 42-43) was regularly visited by Harlow's hermit, Mr Charlie Haddock. He often had pheasants and rabbits for sale that he had shot with his catapult or killed with

HARLOW POTTER STREET

Potter Street, St Mary Magdalene Church c1955 P147009

POTTER STREET

Potter Street, The White Horse c1955 P147001

The White Horse stands on the edge of Harlow Common.

a thick stick. He lived in the old gravel pit by the railway line at Harlow from 1935 until 1957. He had made himself a cave in the side of the pit. It was heated by a coal fire, and was sparsely furnished. It is said that the walls were lined with £5 notes. Charlie seemed to have a regular income, which he collected every month from a London solicitor.

He was very popular in the White Horse, generously treating customers to round after round of drinks. He often talked about his war service in the army, showing

HARLOW POTTER STREET

everyone his medals. As well as a having a fund of good stories, he could talk well on almost any subject. When Charlie was in hospital with pneumonia, vandals broke into his cave and set fire to it. He died soon after, and later, when two of his relatives turned up, it was revealed that Charlie was a fraud. His surname was Skate, he had only been in the army for six days, and the medals weren't his; the reason he had become a hermit was to hide from a girl he had become involved with in Australia.

HARLOW
POTTER STREET

Below: Potter Street, The Junior School c1955 P147010

Potter Street Junior School and the infant school were on the same campus, and were typical of the many schools that had to be provided quickly for the very large percentage of school-age children in Harlow New Town. Later, as the numbers of children decreased, the two schools were amalgamated into a primary school. The local comprehensive school is within easy walking distance along one of the old lanes preserved by the planners.

HARLOW POTTER STREET

Above: POTTER STREET, POTTERSFIELD c1960 P147016

Great care was taken in planning new areas, with safe open spaces where children could play unsupervised. Note the unfenced playground equipment, and the little box on old pram wheels that so many children made, so typical of the time. This development of 178 dwellings was built in 1952-55, so these children will have been able to go to the brand new school in the village.

Left: POTTER STREET, PERRY SPRING c1960 P147033

Perry Spring was a housing area of one hundred and twenty six houses, and included a community centre. Some sculptures, 'Torsos', by Karel Vogel, were sited outside. The centre was to be managed by the Potter Street Residents and Community Association. Landlord and tenant matters were to be dealt with by the residents' committee. This has proved to be one of the most successful associations in Harlow.

HARLOW
ESSEX COUNTY MAP

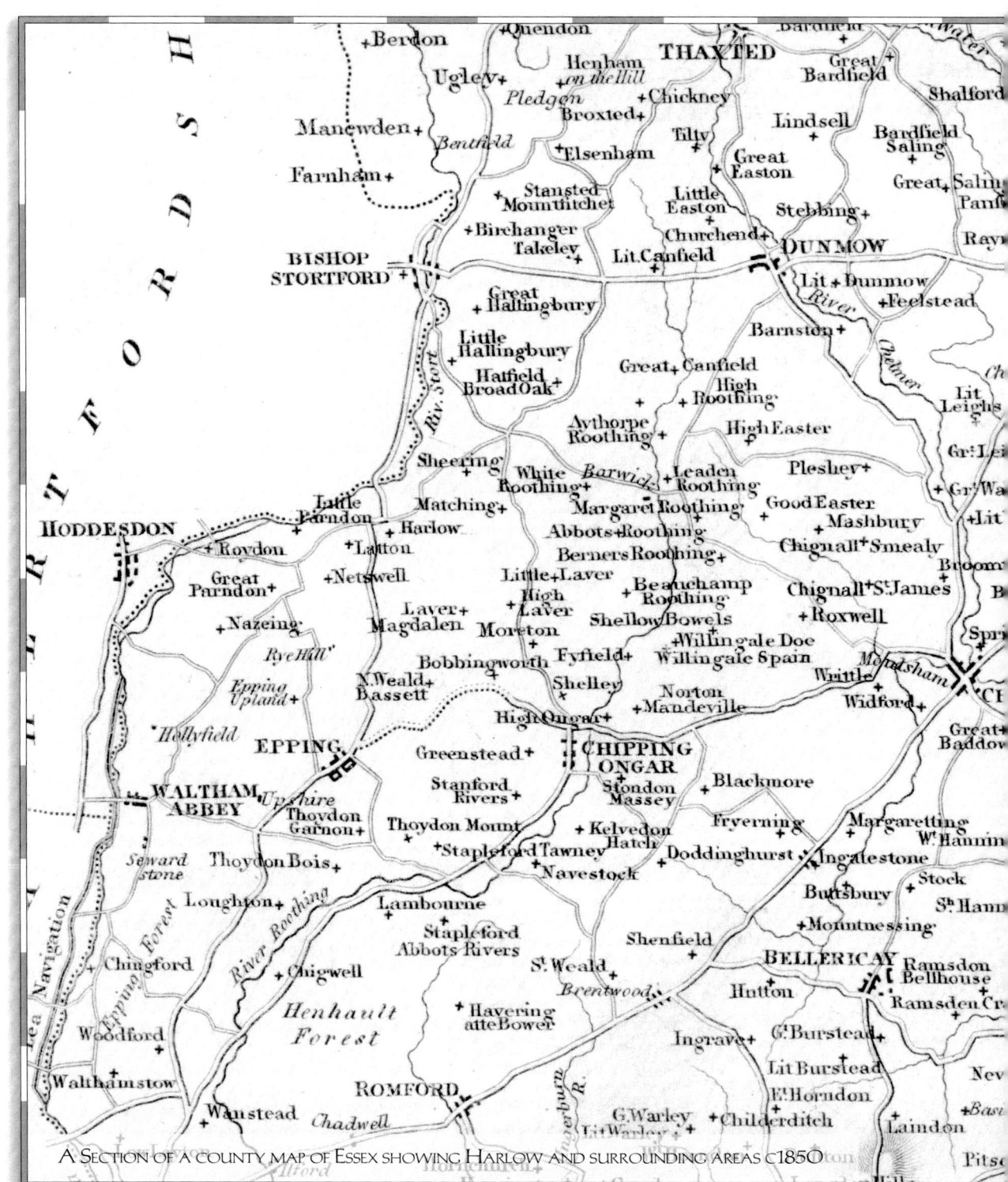

A Section of a county map of Essex showing Harlow and surrounding areas c1850

HARLOW
ESSEX COUNTY MAP

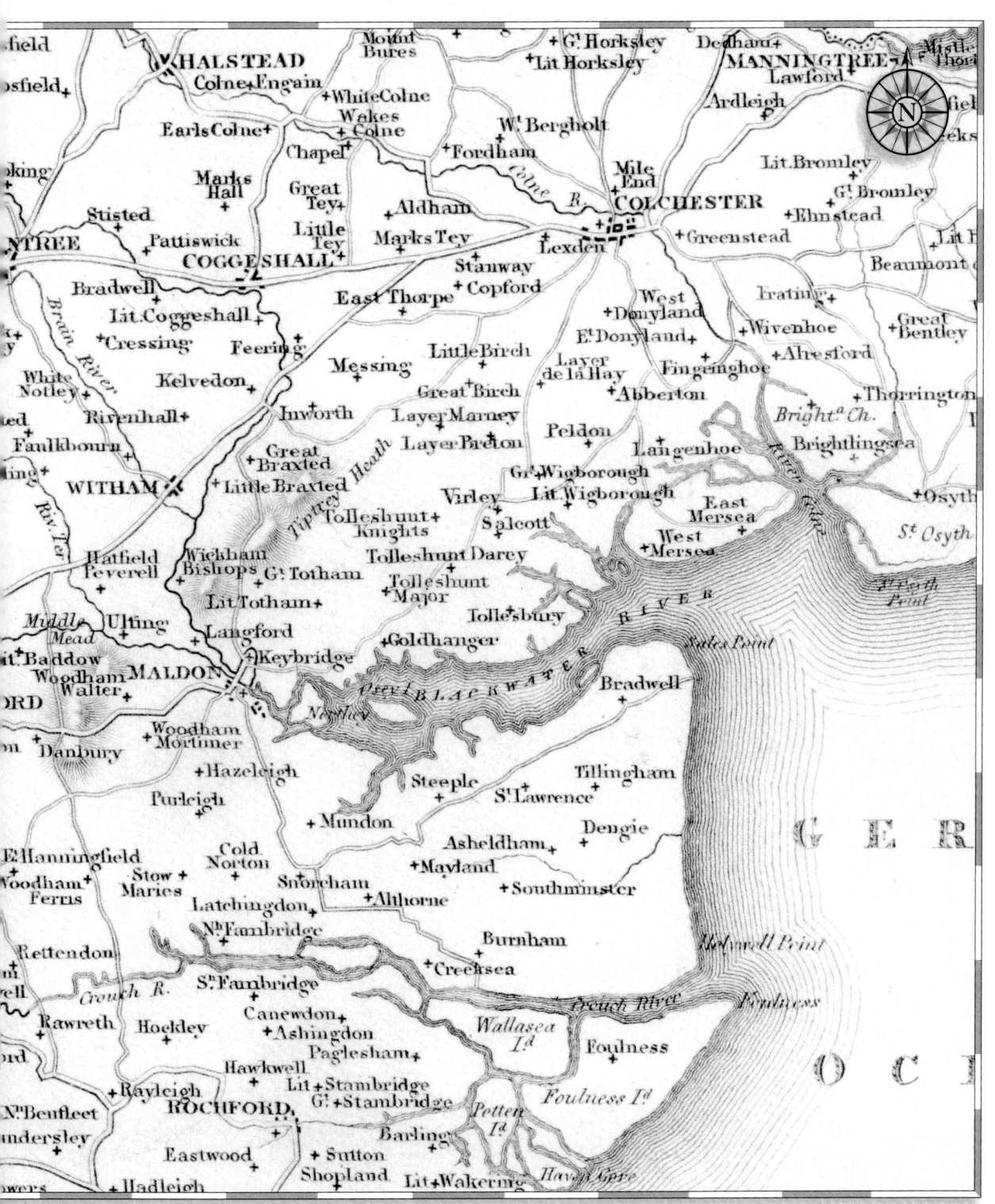

HARLOW
THE NEW TOWN

IN 1946 Frederick Gibberd was informally asked to undertake a design for a new town by Lewis Silkin. The Harlow Development Corporation came into existence in 1947. Harlow was chosen because of its good position, good communications, and quality of landscape.

Harlow will always be protected from urban sprawl by Epping Forest, the Corporation of London's gift to the people of East London. In 1946 London was still ravaged by bomb damage, and the new town could offer not only help with rehousing the homeless, but also a new way of life.

The new town was to be built on the old hamlets of Latton, Netteswell, Great Parndon and Little Parndon.

Wherever possible, the old names of people and places were to be used, and ancient tracks, lanes and bridleways between the hamlets would be kept to link neighbourhood clusters in the New Town, providing safe and easy ways to cycle or walk to work or the shops. The houses were to be allocated only to people working in Harlow, preferably those with required skills. Between 1955 and 1957, houses in Upper Park were built for sale.

FIRST AVENUE C1965 H22132

The New Town was to be beautiful, and to work well, with wide tree-lined roads densely planted with trees and shrubs. The natural landscape was to be kept as linear parks, so that everyone was within walking distance of the countryside.

HARLOW THE NEW TOWN

THE STOW

THE STOW

THE first neighbourhood to be developed was the Mark Hall neighbourhood, with The Stow as its centre. The old vicarage, renamed Moot House (H22028, below) was used as a community centre, library, clinic, information centre and clubhouse for associations and groups.

The dramatic societies and music groups that began here were later to use the Playhouse. Inside are two murals bought from the Festival of Britain, 'Boats' by Alan Sorrell and '1851' by Leonard Manasseh. It was seen as essential to have these kind of activities. The new settlers had left behind family and friends, and some were very lonely and depressed. Having battled with a sea of mud and dust all day, or been at home alone with the children, they needed some kind of light relief.

The shopping area in The Stow (H22044, opposite) has shops with recessed windows and entrances, maisonette living areas, service areas, and community provision to cover most things. The planners disagreed about the road in front of the shops; later, when the traffic became intolerable, the area was pedestrianised.

The first of Harlow's new pubs was opened here in 1952. It is called the Essex Skipper, and it began the tradition of naming all seventeen new pubs in Harlow after butterflies. There were already eight old country pubs in the area, and these were all to be refurbished and conserved.

MOOT HOUSE c1955 H22028

The former vicarage was renamed Moot House, and was used as a busy community centre.

HARLOW THE STOW

THE STOW c1955 H22044

The Stow was to be the New Town's first major shopping centre. The design is Z-shaped, running from north to south to catch as much sunlight as possible, with a square at each end. Moot House, with its mature trees, paved area and sculpture (left), is at one end, while the other square is used for commercial purposes.

MOOT HOUSE AND THE STOW c1960 H22048

The paved area in front of Moot House was a sunny meeting place with mature trees, flower boxes and seats. The sculpture in front of Moot House was one of the first to be given to the town by the Harlow Art Trust. Called 'Chiron', it was bought to commemorate the coronation of Queen Elizabeth II. It is the work of Mary Spencer Watson, and she completed the work on the spot. When the library was built, a bronze statue, 'Boy Eating Apple' by Percy Portsmouth, was sited outside.

HARLOW
TREASURES OF THE PAST

The Round House, Latton Street c1955 H22020

TREASURES OF THE PAST

AGRICULTURAL workers in the 19th century were very poorly paid. However, some were provided with tied cottages, particularly by a local employer and landowner, Reverend Joseph Arkwright.

The Round House (H22020, opposite) was built about 1750 on Latton Street just north of Maypole Corner, near the site of Potter Street's famous Prentice Pottery, which produced England's first ceramic dish. It was a two-up, two-down cottage, and given the large thatched roof and tree trunk supports, was probably designed more for effect than convenience. It was demolished in 1955 when that area of Harlow New Town was being developed. There is an existing example of this kind of house in Finchingfield.

The conservation programme included in the new town plan included the churches in the original villages. Population changes meant that some of them were redundant.

ST MARY THE VIRGIN

St Mary The Virgin at Great Parndon (G97001, page 54) stands on an ancient site. The first rector, Geoffrey De Parndon, held office at the church in 1198. In the mid 15th century the building in use today was erected, replacing, or reconstructing, the earlier church. The chancel, nave, tower and vestry were part of the rebuilding, together with the Perpendicular-style windows. The piscina, a shallow stone basin, and carved stone font both date from the 15th-century as do the benches with characteristic 'poppy heads'

GREAT PARNDON, THE COCK INN C1960 G97004

The Cock Inn at Cock Green, Great Parndon, is thought to be one of the oldest pubs in Harlow; it dates from the Stuart period. It was an important link in the coach transport network, and it would have provided stabling and change of horses as well as refreshment in the 17th and 18th centuries. The brewers before Barclay Perkins were Chaplins of Old Harlow. They did not send malt and barley to London, but made their own ales and stout, selling it locally.

at both ends. The 15th-century doorway was bricked up long ago but its shape can be seen on the outside wall of the church. The South Transept was added in the 16th century, and the North Transept in 1913. There have been stained glass windows in the church from the 15th century onwards. The Jubilee Window commemorating the Silver Jubilee of Queen Elizabeth II (1952-1977) was a gift from St Mary's (Great Parndon) Preservation Society. In 1958 three of the bells, first installed in 1613 and 1779, were restored and rehung. The fourth, a tenor, was cast in 1613 and is in its original state. In 1967 there was a comprehensive restoration of the tower, with repointing of its old rubble walls, and repairs to the windows and clock.

There are 17th- and 18th-century memorial tablets in marble and alabaster, and a memorial brass from 1598. Gifts of money, furniture, and a new floor from parishioners, all keep this beautiful old church in good repair.

GREAT PARNDON, THE CHURCH OF ST MARY THE VIRGIN C1960 G97001

There has been a church here since 1198. The pews, windows, a font, a piscina, and many parts of the church date from that time. The church in the photograph was a reconstruction and rebuilding of the original building.

HARLOW TREASURES OF THE PAST

ST MARY-AT-LATTON

The Domesday Book records a wooden Saxon church with a tower that was built on this site about 900. In 1087 the Normans built a stone church using some of the Roman brick from a 3rd-century ancient Roman temple in the parish. There are three excellent brass effigies of the Arderne family from the 15th century in the church. Marks of the Norman doorway can be seen over the porch built in 1562 by the wealthy Altham family, who endowed the church with some silver plate. They also had the present tower built, complete with bells. A gift of a barrel of beer to the bell ringers in 1641 led to a violent disagreement about some newly erected rails between the sanctuary and the nave, and they chopped up and burnt. An altar frontal embroidered by Mary Altham in about 1705 was found in an attic at Moot House and is now in Harlow Museum. In the early 20th century the parish declined drastically and in 1950 the church was derelict. A group of people got together and the church was reopened and reconsecrated. Slowly but surely the church was repaired and restored to become the warm and welcoming place it is today.

HARLOW, ST MARY-AT-LATTON c1960 H22055

A wooden Saxon church was built on site in 900. There was a 3rd-century Roman temple in the parish and the next church, built by the Norman in 1087, included rubble and brick from the ruins. In the 20th century the parish declined and the church became almost unused. In 1950 a group of people decided to reopen the derelict church. It was reconsecrated in 1950 and since then restoration and care have restored it to its former beauty.

THE NEIGHBOURHOOD CLUSTERS

THE plan was to build houses grouped around a major shopping and social centre. Each of the thirteen housing areas were to be individually designed. Some of the designs were very advanced for their time, but they have since become very popular. There was an emphasis on quality, both in the design and the materials.

The housing was to be of good quality and innovative design, and suitable for all ages and circumstances. Large businesses and small workshops were planned, all to be within walking or cycling distance of the shops or place of employment. Later, some of the Corporation houses were offered to tenants to buy. Harlow was to consist of several housing areas, each with its own centre containing a shopping area, a community centre, a school, and a church. The housing areas were linked by old lanes, which were to be used as cycle paths or footpaths. Wherever possible, existing buildings were restored and made part of the new neighbourhood.

By 1956, the Corporation had built over seventy factories and more than seven thousand dwellings. The Town Centre had started trading, and an open air market began on Whit Monday 1956. In the New Town, car ownership was beginning to cause problems. The planners realised that the bicycle town idea was no longer viable, and that all the houses built up till then would need garage space. Odd bits of ground and some infilling was used to increase the garaging and parking areas. The design used for Orchard Croft (H22029, pages 58) was a new approach and was designed to have integral garages. The town house design has a garage on the ground floor with the living area above. The design received a lot of publicity and a Ministry of Housing award.

Two semi-detached houses in The Chantry (H22030, page 59) were adapted for use as a temporary health centre. The plan was to provide all medical services under one roof. This was a new idea, and the success of the project led to the development of similar health centres in other parts of the town, and throughout the world.

FELMONGERS C1955 H22033

Felmongers was begun in 1950, and not finished until 1956. The early settlers had to battle with endless mud and builders' mess. The houses were designed by Featherstone, and were very attractive with white walls and dark roofs. Wherever possible, mature trees were kept, and if necessary new ones were planted.

THE NEIGHBOURHOOD CLUSTERS

THE LAWN TOWER BLOCK c1955 H22018

This nine-storey block was a typical example of housing seen as being ideal for single people. The first one was built on the corner of Mark Hall Moors in open parkland in the midst of seven magnificent oaks. It was designed in the shape of a butterfly, so that the sitting rooms look south over the landscape. It received a Festival of Britain award.

HARLOW
THE NEIGHBOURHOOD CLUSTERS

SHARPECROFT C1955 H22034

Sharpecroft was started in 1955 and finished one year later.

ORCHARD CROFT C1955 H22029

The name Orchard Croft was taken from an old tithe map of the area. Orchard Croft includes flats and the so-called 'banana blocks' that face the cricket field, and was given Grade II status in 1992.

THE NEIGHBOURHOOD CLUSTERS

The Chantry c1955 H22030

HARLOW
THE TOWN CENTRE

Above: WEST WALK c1965 H22095

West Walk was reserved for banks, solicitors, estate agents, a cinema, and small specialist shops.

THE TOWN CENTRE

THE TOWN CENTRE

PLANS for the town centre were simple. There was a rectangular layout, with the shops in the middle, and the bus terminus along one side; West Walk (H22095, opposite) along the other side, was reached through a wide walkway called Little Walk. The market square was at one end, and the library and civic square at the other, and there was a walkway to the Bus Terminus opposite West Walk.

By 1956 the Town Centre had started trading. National multiples such as Boots, Sainsbury's, the Co-op, Dolcis and WH Smith opened in 1958; Marks and Spencer followed in 1969. These popular retailers attracted people from surrounding villages and towns as well as all the young families in Harlow New Town.

The number of prams and push-chairs in Harlow gave rise to its nickname 'Pram Town' (see H22083, pages 62-63). By the 1960s the number of prams and bicycles had diminished, and seats had been placed in Broad Walk (H22113, pages 64). To make the Walk more interesting, display boxes were put at intervals down the middle (H22099, pages 64-65). The idea was that local businesses would display beautiful examples of their work in them. After a few disasters, good design became a feature of the exhibits, but for financial reasons they were finally scrapped. Much later, when the Harvey Centre was built, Little Walk (between Broad Walk and West Walk) was given a glass roof (H22097, page 65). In 1978 the Arts Council made a grant towards a sculpture by Paul Mason in Broad Walk. The Obelisk was paid for by the Harlow Development Corporation to commemorate the building of the town.

TERMINUS STREET c1960 H22082

Local bus services used Terminus Street, and so did the Green Line and National Express. The furniture and furnishing shops were all concentrated in this area.

HARLOW
THE TOWN CENTRE

HARLOW THE TOWN CENTRE

Broad Walk c1960 H22083

One of the busiest shops in Broad Walk was Bellmans, selling wool and patterns for babies and young children. Many people went to the Town Centre on bicycles, and left them leaning against the wall opposite the shops.

HARLOW
THE TOWN CENTRE

Broad Walk c1965 H22099

Broad Walk c1965 H22113

HARLOW THE TOWN CENTRE

Little Walk c1965 H22097

THE MARKET SQUARE

PROPOSALS for a Market Square were strongly opposed by some members of the Development Corporation. Sir Frederick Gibberd envisaged a market area with stalls for small traders from Harlow and outside the town who could not afford shop rents.

Some members of the Corporation thought that his ideas 'would produce an element of brash vulgarity', but later, having seen the Lansbury market in Stepney which was similar to the one proposed for Harlow, were finally prepared to let it go ahead. The market began trading in 1956 with forty-six stalls on Tuesdays and Saturdays, and later on Thursdays and Fridays. Prince Philip had been to Harlow when it was a sea of mud. The Queen came to the Market Square in 1957 soon after it had been completed.

There were several entrances to the square. Post Office Walk consisted of service shops, and the entrance from the south (H22037, page 68) had larger shops selling electrical goods and some small businesses.

Cars and bicycles used to park between Broad Walk and Market Square (H22050, pages 68-69). This was a through road for several years. Car ownership increased dramatically, and later the road was closed to traffic. The Harlow Art Trust commissioned

HARLOW THE MARKET SQUARE

Market House c1955 H22035

THE MARKET SQUARE

a cast bronze sculpture by Ralph Brown called 'The Meat Porters' and this, together with 'Portrait Figure' by F E McWilliam, was placed in the market square (H22103, page 70).

By 1965 the town had grown, with many more public buildings. The Terminus area was now a major coach and bus terminus (H22115, below).

Market House c1955 H22037

There were to be three types of shopping: the open-air market, a variety of shops on three sides, and a first-floor row of shops that did not need a window display, such as hairdressers, opticians, photographers, and a restaurant overlooking the market, with bridges, stairs and terraces between.

Terminus Street c1965 H22115

HARLOW THE MARKET SQUARE

Market Square and Broad Walk c1960 H22050

HARLOW
THE MARKET SQUARE

THE STATUE C1965 H22103

'The Meat Porters', a cast bronze structure by Ralph Brown, was commissioned by the Harlow Art Trust. It was a popular choice and has been in the Market Square since 1960.

THE RAILWAY - HARLOW STATION

THE RAILWAY first reached Harlow Mill (formerly called Harlow) in 1841. Very soon after, in 1844, the broad (7ft) railway tracks had to be replaced by a narrow gauge (44ft 8½ inches) that was becoming standard nation-wide. The company had planned, unsuccessfully, to extend the line to York. The railway brought industry to the area, but it had a bad effect on the canal trade, coach services and innkeepers. The coaching business run by the Gilbey family collapsed, and they changed to dealing in wine (Gilbeys became a major employer in Harlow New Town).

In the 1920s a local businessman, Mr Charles Scruby, could see other opportunities from the new railway; he proposed to develop an estate of houses, called Harlow Garden Village, for people prepared to commute to London. The Scruby family built Priory Avenue and properties in Old Road. They did not achieve the Garden village, but instead built a number of bungalows. After the railway came to Old Harlow, the canal was no longer used to transport goods to London. In 1911 all the directors in Lee Conservancy sold their interests in the canal. The locks and the waterway gradually became unusable, and it was not until 1924 that repairs to the locks were completed and the canal reopened. Up until 1955 barges used the canal commercially.

Harlow New Station was opened in 1961. Harlow Mill serves the eastern side of the New Town, and Old Harlow. The New Town was planned to provide jobs within the town, all within easy reach by bicycle, so train services were sparse. Most of the people who had moved to

THE STATION C1960 H22080

The Stansted Skytrain now operates through Harlow, and the rail network links with the Channel Tunnel's Eurostar service to provide a route into mainland Europe.

THE RAILWAY - HARLOW STATION

Harlow were from London, and had left behind families and friends that they wanted to visit at the weekend. There were many complaints about the frequency of the service, and British Rail increased the number of trains at the weekend, but not during the week. Local industries were reluctant to use the railway. They complained that there was 'no certainty of delivery time, losses and damage'. United Glass Works were the exception - they used the freight trains for transporting sand.

The population in 1960 was 50,000, yet in photograph H22080 there are only about 60 cars parked at the station, as most people worked in the town. Nowadays there has been a dramatic increase in car ownership and commuting, as many of the local companies have closed down. Both Harlow Mill and Harlow New Town station are used daily by commuters to London and Cambridge.

NEW TOWN STATION C1960 H22066

The station is just a few yards from the site of the little gas-lit halt of Burnt Mill. Until 1960 the first New Town settlers used the halt, huddling in a tiny porter's hut on cold mornings, warmed by a small coal stove. It was demolished in 1960.

THE RAILWAY - HARLOW STATION

THE CIVIC CENTRE

THE CIVIC CENTRE

THE STATUE AND THE TOWN HALL c1965 H22088

The Town Hall, opened in 1960 by Clement Attlee, is part of a group of buildings in the Civic Centre. The sculpture is 'Bronze Cross', by Henry Moore, and was placed in the water gardens.

HARLOW THE CIVIC CENTRE

The Water Gardens c1965 H22121

The sculpture 'Eve' by Rodin was placed at the far end one of the water canals.

THE CIVIC CENTRE

THE COUNTY CONSTABULARY c1960 H22062

The police station and the magistrates' courts were designed by Frederick Gibberd and completed in 1959.

JUST behind the Town Hall (H22086, opposite) is the Civic Square. This was intended to be 'the most splendid space in the town, the equivalent of the Piazza San Marco in Venice'. The Art Trust commissioned 'The Family Group', a sculpture by Henry Moore, and it was originally sited in a grassed area near St Mary-at-Latton Church. It was later moved to Civic Square and in 2002 moved to the Civic Centre. Some sculptures were kept in the Gibberd Gardens pending the rebuilding of the water gardens surrounding the shopping centre.

Everything in the town was within easy reach, including the shops, the Town Hall, buses, car parks, government offices, the library, the police station and quiet areas to sit in. Large sites around the Town Centre rectangle were for the fire station, built in 1957, the sports stadium, built in 1960, the swimming pool, built in 1961, and a helicopter landing pad.

The water gardens (H22086, opposite) are between the Town Centre and one of the car parks. Behind the car park is an uninterrupted view of one of the landscape wedges where the countryside had been kept between the neighbourhood clusters. The water gardens step down from the civic centre in three levels planted with flowers and shrubs. From a canal at the top, water is delivered through seven lions' heads (designed by William Mitchell) to a central canal, then piped to pools in small enclosed gardens at the lowest level. 'Eve', a bronze by Rodin, was placed at the far end of one of the water canals.

HARLOW THE CIVIC CENTRE

Above: THE WATER GARDENS AND THE TOWN HALL c1965 H22086

Left: DETAIL OF H22086

HARLOW
NEW CHURCHES AND PUBLIC BUILDINGS

NEW CHURCHES AND PUBLIC BUILDINGS

ST PAUL'S CHURCH, THE INTERIOR c1960 H22058
This shows the interior of St Paul's Church, with the mural by John Piper behind the altar.

NEW CHURCHES AND PUBLIC BUILDINGS

ST PAUL'S parish church (H22054, page 80) was built in 1959. The surrounding buildings are clad in pre-cast concrete and Cornish granite (H22109, pages 80-81); as the church is a small building, and in order to contrast with its surroundings, it was clad in brick. It was designed by Derrick Humphrys. It is notable for its brightly-coloured furnishings and a mural by John Piper behind the altar (H22058, opposite); there is also a stone carving called Madonna and Child, whose origin is unknown. The little building at the side of St Paul's is a bell tower and an open pulpit in front of a small paved area.

The Catholic church of Our Lady Fatima was opened in 1960 (H22129, page 80). It has a huge stained glass window depicting saints, which was made by the monks of Buckfast Abbey using a new technique of pre-fabricated panels of cast glass and concrete. The spire was made elsewhere and then placed in position by helicopter.

The site the hospital stands on (H22125, page 82) was once the home of Loftus Wigram Arkwright, great-grandson of Sir Richard Arkwright, the inventor who triggered off the industrial revolution. The Arkwright family have an important place in Harlow's history.

HARLOW
NEW CHURCHES AND PUBLIC BUILDINGS

The family first moved to the area sometime in 1819, when Arkwright bought Mark Hall, and for the next 150 years managed and enlarged their estate.

The River Stort became badly polluted by the growing population and industrial effluent, but this has been cleaned up by the new sewage works and better disposal of industrial waste. The river can now provide facilities for a canoe club, boating and angling. The swimming pool building (H22128, page 82) which also offers fitness and well-being courses, attracts people from surrounding towns and villages.

The biggest and most important of the linear parks is the Town Park. It has no hard boundaries, but is bounded along one side by the River Stort. There is a small area of land on the other side of the Stort, and this enables walkers to follow the Harcamlow Way. In 1955 it was not clear whether the river would be used commercially, so at first only a riverside walk was proposed.

The well-maintained path by the River Stort (H22022, page 83) could be used by walkers, cyclists and fishermen. Later, when it became clear that the river could be used for sport and leisure, both the county and the District Councils developed centres for water sports. There has been a growth in the use of narrow boats for holidays, for floating restaurants, and to live in.

THE CHURCH OF OUR LADY FATIMA c1965 H22129

THE PARISH CHURCH OF ST PAUL c1960 H22054

NEW CHURCHES AND PUBLIC BUILDINGS

The Town Centre c1965 H22109

This aerial view of the Town Centre shows the wide roads threading through the landscape wedges. St Paul's Church was designed to contrast with the building styles of the large buildings around it.

Below: Detail of H22054

HARLOW
NEW CHURCHES AND PUBLIC BUILDINGS

The Princess Alexandra Hospital c1965 H22125

The greater part of the land needed for Harlow New Town was owned by Godfrey Arkwright, and he sold it to the Development Corporation in 1953. His home, Parndon Hall, has been retained in the grounds of Princess Alexandra Hospital, and is now used as offices for the hospital.

The Swimming Pool c1965 H22128

Harlow swimming pool is on the south edge of the Town Park. The site is about half a mile from the part of the River Stort that had been used for swimming lessons and galas by local schools for at least one hundred years.

NEW CHURCHES AND PUBLIC BUILDINGS

THE PADDLING POOL c1965 H22127

Families with small children could always come to one of the many paddling pools in the area. The pool setting is designed so that a whole day could be spent there, with grassy banks for having a picnic and open spaces in which to run about.

THE BRIDGE AT OLD HARLOW, NEAR HARLOW MILL c1955 H22022

HARLOW
NEW CHURCHES AND PUBLIC BUILDINGS

HARLOW
NEW CHURCHES AND PUBLIC BUILDINGS

Burnt Mill Lock House and Bridge c1955 H22024

The River Stort c1955 H22012

The River Stort, with the Town Park along its banks, has become a beautiful and popular venue for the people of Harlow, Old and New.

Names of Subscribers

The following people have kindly supported this book by purchasing limited edition copies prior to publication.

Aldridge and Agnes Family

Amy Louise Barnard

Brandon - your town

The Brett Family, Harlow

To Brian, in memory of our parents

James Henry Clarke

In Memory of the artist A I Cowen

In memory of Ronald C Cox 1913 - 1965

To Brian Finch, Harlow on his 65th Birthday

Mrs D Gibson

Miss Gillian Gorham for Mr and Mrs B Gorham

Harlow Citizen

Heath Harrington from Edmonton, Harlow

Ray and Dawn Hicks

To my precious daughter Jayne, love Dad

The Kearney Family, Church Langley

The Shujat Ali Khan Family, Harlow

The Morgans Family, Harlow

To Mum on your 65th birthday with love

In memory of my parents

To Teddy (Monty) Rumelhart, Harlow

To Sandra, in memory of our parents

Ron Smeeton, resident in Harlow since 1952

Edwin and Veronica Steel, Harlow, from Rob

Chris S Stevens

Michael, Barbara and John Stiles, Harlow

Wieslaw Tobolewski and family, Harlow

In memory of my father Stanley B Ward

Wen and Alan, love Ros and John

Cyril and Eileen Whitehead, A life together

The Wright Family of Harlow

In memory of Mary Martina Wright, Harlow

INDEX

Bridge at Old Harlow 83
Broad Walk 62-63, 64-65, 68-69
Burnt Mill Lock House and Bridge ... 84-85
The Chantry 59
Church of Our Lady Fatima 80
Church of St Mary the Virgin 54
County Constabulary 76
Felmongers 56
First Avenue 48-49
Great Parndon 53, 54
Lawn Tower Block 57
Little Walk 65
Market House 66-67, 68
Market Square and Broad Walk 68-69
The Mill 14-15
Moot House 50
Moot House and The Stow 51
New Town Station 72-73
Orchard Croft 58
Paddling Pool 83
Potter Street 38-39, 40-41, 42-43, 44-45
Princess Alexandra Hospital 82
River Stort 2, 84-85
Round House 52
Sharpecroft 58-59
St Mary-at-Latton 55
St Mary Magdalene Church 40-41

St Paul's Church 80
St Paul's Church, The Interior 78-79
Station 71
The Statue 'The Meat Porters' 70
The Statue 'Bronze Cross'
  and the Town Hall 74
The Stow 51
Swimming Pool 82
Terminus Street 60-61, 68
Town Hall 74, 77
Town Centre 80-81
Water Gardens 74-75, 77
West Walk 60-61
White Horse 42-43

OLD HARLOW

Chippingfield Housing Area 34-35
Church of St Mary and St Hugh 12-13
Churchgate Street 11, 12
College 21, 22-23
The Ford 26-27
The George 20
The Green 30-31
High Street 18-19
Mulberry Green 24-25
Old Harlow Cottages 16-17
Post Office Corner 32-33

FRITH PRODUCTS & SERVICES

Francis Frith would doubtless be pleased to know that the pioneering publishing venture he started in 1860 still continues today. Over a hundred and forty years later, The Francis Frith Collection continues in the same innovative tradition and is now one of the foremost publishers of vintage photographs in the world. Some of the current activities include:

INTERIOR DECORATION
Today Frith's photographs can be seen framed and as giant wall murals in thousands of pubs, restaurants, hotels, banks, retail stores and other public buildings throughout the country. In every case they enhance the unique local atmosphere of the places they depict and provide reminders of gentler days in an increasingly busy and frenetic world.

PRODUCT PROMOTIONS
Frith products are used by many major companies to promote the sales of their own products or to reinforce their own history and heritage. Frith promotions have been used by Hovis bread, Courage beers, Scots Porage Oats, Colman's mustard, Cadbury's foods, Mellow Birds coffee, Dunhill pipe tobacco, Guinness, and Bulmer's Cider.

GENEALOGY AND FAMILY HISTORY
As the interest in family history and roots grows world-wide, more and more people are turning to Frith's photographs of Great Britain for images of the towns, villages and streets where their ancestors lived; and, of course, photographs of the churches and chapels where their ancestors were christened, married and buried are an essential part of every genealogy tree and family album.

FRITH PRODUCTS
All Frith photographs are available Framed or just as Mounted Prints and unmounted versions. These may be ordered from the address below. Other products available are - Calendars, Jigsaws, Canvas Prints, Mugs, Tea Towels, Tableware and local and prestige books.

THE INTERNET
Over several hundred thousand Frith photographs can be viewed and purchased on the internet through the Frith websites!

For more detailed information on Frith products, look at
www.francisfrith.com

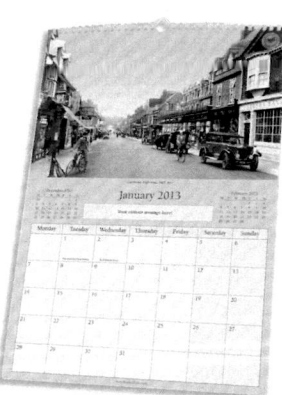

See the complete list of Frith Books at: www.francisfrith.com
This web site is regularly updated with the latest list of publications from The Francis Frith Collection. If you wish to buy books relating to another part of the country that your local bookshop does not stock, you may purchase on-line.

For further information, trade, or author enquiries please contact us at the address below:
The Francis Frith Collection, Unit 19 Kingsmead Business Park, Gillingham, Dorset SP8 5FB.
Tel: +44 (0)1722 716 376   Email: sales@francisfrith.co.uk

See Frith products on the internet at www.francisfrith.com

FREE PRINT OF YOUR CHOICE
CHOOSE A PHOTOGRAPH FROM THIS BOOK

+ POSTAGE

Mounted Print
Overall size 14 x 11 inches (355 x 280mm)

TO RECEIVE YOUR FREE PRINT

Choose any Frith photograph in this book
Simply complete the Voucher opposite and return it with your payment (to cover postage and handling) and we will print the photograph of your choice in SEPIA (size 11 x 8 inches) and supply it in a cream mount ready to frame (overall size 14 x 11 inches).

Order additional Mounted Prints at HALF PRICE - £19.00 each (normally £38.00)
If you would like to order more Frith prints from this book, possibly as gifts for friends and family, you can buy them at half price (with no additional postage costs).

Have your Mounted Prints framed
For an extra £20.00 per print you can have your mounted print(s) framed in an elegant polished wood and gilt moulding, overall size 16 x 13 inches (no additional postage required).

IMPORTANT!

❶ Please note: aerial photographs and photographs with a reference number starting with a "Z" are not Frith photographs and cannot be supplied under this offer.

❷ Offer valid for delivery to one UK address only.

❸ These special prices are only available if you use this form to order. You must use the ORIGINAL VOUCHER on this page (no copies permitted). We can only despatch to one UK address.

❹ This offer cannot be combined with any other offer.

As a customer your name & address will be stored by Frith but not sold or rented to third parties. Your data will be used for the purpose of this promotion only.

Send completed Voucher form to:
**The Francis Frith Collection,
1 Chilmark Estate House, Chilmark,
Salisbury, Wiltshire SP3 5DU**

Voucher
for FREE and Reduced Price Frith Prints

Please do not photocopy this voucher. Only the original is valid, so please fill it in, cut it out and return it to us with your order.

Picture ref no	Page no	Qty	Mounted @ £19.00	Framed + £20.00	Total Cost £
		1	Free of charge*	£	£
			£19.00	£	£
			£19.00	£	£
			£19.00	£	£
			£19.00	£	£
			£19.00	£	£
Please allow 28 days for delivery. Offer available to one UK address only			* Post & handling		£3.80
			Total Order Cost		£

Title of this book ....

I enclose a cheque/postal order for £ ....

made payable to 'Heritage Resource Management Ltd'

OR please debit my Mastercard / Visa / Maestro card, details below

Card Number:

Issue No (Maestro only):   Valid from (Maestro):

Card Security Number: Expires:

Signature:

Name Mr/Mrs/Ms ....

Address ....

....

....

.... Postcode ....

Daytime Tel No ....

Email ....

Valid to 31/12/26

Free Print – see overleaf

Can you help us with information about any of the Frith photographs in this book?

We are gradually compiling an historical record for each of the photographs in the Frith archive. It is always fascinating to find out the names of the people shown in the pictures, as well as insights into the shops, buildings and other features depicted.

If you recognize anyone in the photographs in this book, or if you have information not already included in the author's caption, do let us know. We would love to hear from you, and will try to publish it in future books or articles.

An Invitation from The Francis Frith Collection to Share Your Memories

The 'Share Your Memories' feature of our website allows members of the public to add personal memories relating to the places featured in our photographs, or comment on others already added. Seeing a place from your past can rekindle forgotten or long held memories. Why not visit the website, find photographs of places you know well and add YOUR story for others to read and enjoy? We would love to hear from you!

www.francisfrith.com/memories

Our production team

Frith books are produced by a small dedicated team at offices near Salisbury. Most have worked with the Frith Collection for many years. All have in common one quality: they have a passion for the Frith Collection.

Frith Books and Gifts

We have a wide range of books and gifts available on our website utilising our photographic archive, many of which can be individually personalised.

www.francisfrith.com